4-CHORD KEYBOARD SONGBOOK

BEATLES

WISE PUBLICATIONS
part of The Music Sales Group

London/New York/Paris/Sydney/Copenhagen/Berlin/Madrid/Tokyo

Published by:
Wise Publications,
14-15 Berners Street, London W1T 3LJ, UK.

Exclusive Distributors:
Music Sales Limited,
Distribution Centre, Newmarket Road, Bury St Edmunds, Suffolk IP33 3YB, UK.
Music Sales Pty Limited,
120 Rothschild Avenue, Rosebery, NSW 2018, Australia.

Order No. NO91212
ISBN 978-1-84772-495-3
This book © Copyright 2008 Wise Publications,
a division of Music Sales Limited.

Edited by Jessica Williams.
'If You've Got Trouble' arranged by Vasco Hexel.
All music processed by Paul Ewers Music Design.

Printed in the EU.

Your Guarantee of Quality
As publishers, we strive to produce every book to the highest
commercial standards.

The music has been freshly engraved and the book has been carefully designed
to minimise awkward page turns and to make playing from it a real pleasure.

Particular care has been given to specifying acid-free, neutral-sized
paper made from pulps which have not been elemental chlorine bleached.

This pulp is from farmed sustainable forests and was produced with
special regard for the environment.

Throughout, the printing and binding have been planned to ensure
a sturdy, attractive publication which should give years of enjoyment.

If your copy fails to meet our high standards, please inform us
and we will gladly replace it.

www.musicsales.com

IF YOU'VE GOT TROUBLE

Words & Music by John Lennon & Paul McCartney

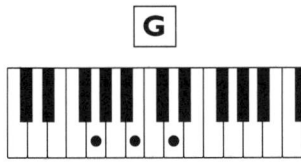

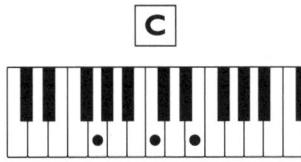

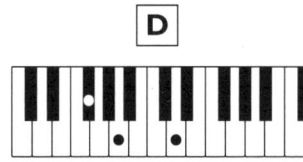

Voice: **Electric Guitar**

Rhythm: **Beat Rock**

Tempo: ♩ = 145

1. If you've got trou - ble then you've got less trou - ble than

me._____ You say you're wor - ried, you

can't be as wor - ried as me,_____ oh, oh._____

You're quite_ con - tent to_ be bad, with all_ the ad - van - tage_ you've

had ov - er me,_ just 'cause you're trou - bled, then don't bring your trou - bles to me.___

2. I don't think it's fun-ny when

you ask for mo-ney and things.___

E-special-ly when you're stand-ing there wear-ing dia-monds and rings,___ oh, oh.

___ You think I'm soft in___ the head well,

try some-one soft-er___ in-stead, pret-ty thing,___ it's not so fun-ny when

you know what mo-ney can bring.___

You bet-ter leave me a-lone,___ I don't need___ a

thing from you,___ you bet-ter take your-self home,___

go and count_ a ring or two._ 3. If you've got trou-ble then

you've got less trou-ble than me._

You say you're wor-ried, you can't be as wor-ried as me,_ oh, oh._

_ You're quite_ con-tent to_ be bad,

with all__ the ad-van-tage_ you've had ov-er me,_

just 'cause you're trou-bled, then don't bring your trou-bles to me._

Just 'cause you're trou-bled, then

don't bring your trou-bles to me._

5

ALL TOGETHER NOW

Words & Music by John Lennon & Paul McCartney

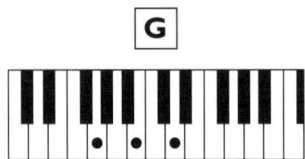

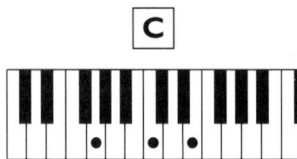

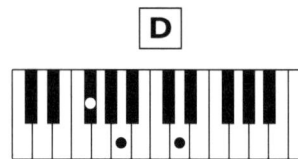

Voice: **Harmonica**

Rhythm: **Shuffle Rock**

Tempo: ♩ = 94

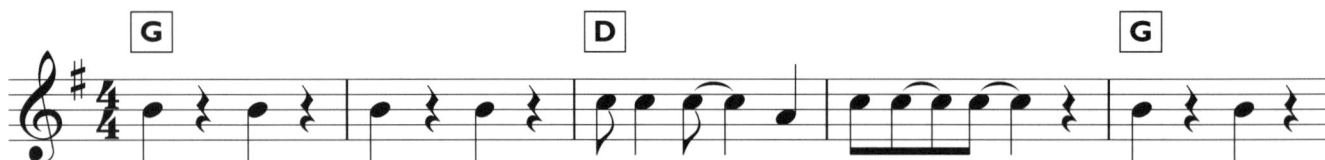

1. One, two, three, four, can I have a lit-tle more? Five, six,
2. A, B, C, D, can I bring my friend to tea? E, F,

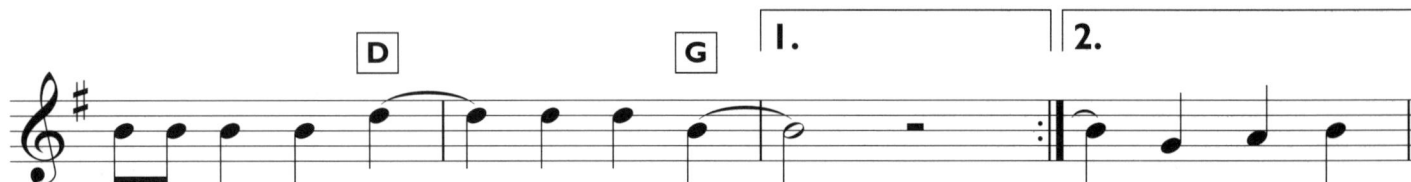

sev-en, eight, nine, ten, I love you.
G, H, I, J, I love you. (Boom boom boom

boom boom boom.) Sail the ship, (boom boom boom.) Chop the tree, (boom boom boom.)

To Coda ⊕

Skip the rope, (boom boom boom.) Look at me! (All to-ge-ther now.)

All to-ge-ther now, (all to-ge-ther now.) All to-ge-ther now, (all to-ge-ther now.)

All to-ge-ther now, (all to-ge-ther now.) All to-ge-ther now.

3. Black, white, green, red, can I take my friend to bed?

Pink, brown, yel-low, or-ange and blue, I love you. (All to - ge-ther now.)

All to - ge - ther now, (all to - ge - ther now.) All to - ge - ther

now, (all to - ge - ther now.) All to - ge - ther now, (all to - ge - ther now.)

1.

All to - ge - ther now, (all to - ge - ther now.)

2. *D.S. al Coda*

now. (Boom boom boom

Coda

gradually getting faster

All to-ge - ther now, (all to-ge-ther now.) All to-ge - ther now, (all to-ge-ther now.)

1, 2.

All to - ge - ther now, (all to-ge-ther now.) All to - ge - ther now, (all to-ge-ther now.)

3.

All to - ge - ther now.

THE BALLAD OF JOHN AND YOKO

Words & Music by John Lennon & Paul McCartney

Voice: **Steel Guitar**

Rhythm: **Blues Rock**

Tempo: ♩ = 138

1. Stand - ing in the dock at South - amp - ton,
2. Final - ly made the plane in - to Pa - ris,

(Verses 3-5 see block lyrics)

trying to get to Hol - land or France.____ The
hon - ey - moon - ing down by the Seine.____ Pe - ter

man in the mac____ said____ "You've got to go back;"____ you know they
Brown called to say____ "You can make it O K;____ you can get

did - n't ev - en give us a chance.____ } Christ! You know it ain't ea -
mar - ried in Gib - ral - tar, near Spain."____

- sy,____ you know how hard it can be.____

To Coda ⊕

The way things are go - ing,___ they're gon - na cru - ci - fy___

1, 4. **2.** **3.**

me. 3. Drove from

Sav - ing up your mon - ey for a rain - y day,___ giv - ing all___ your clothes to cha - ri -

-ty. Last night the wife said, "Oh boy, when you're dead you

D.S. al Coda
(with repeat)

don't take no - thing with you but your soul."_____ Think!

⊕ **Coda**

me. The way things are go - ing___

they're gon - na cru - ci - fy_____ me.

Verse 3:
Paris to the Amsterdam Hilton,
Talking in our beds for a week.
The newspeople said, "Say, what you doing in bed?"
I said, "We're only trying to get us some peace."

Verse 4:
Made a lightning trip to Vienna,
Eating chocolate cake in a bag.
The newspapers said, "She's gone to his head;
They look just like two gurus in drag."

Verse 5:
Caught the early plane back to London,
Fifty acorns tied in a sack.
The men from the press said "We wish you success,
It's good to have the both of you back."

9

DRIVE MY CAR

Words & Music by John Lennon & Paul McCartney

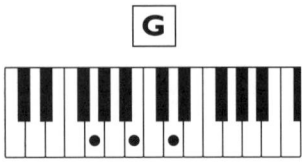

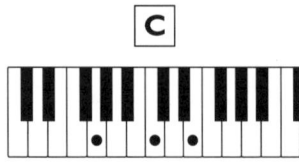

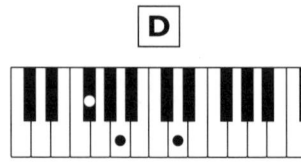

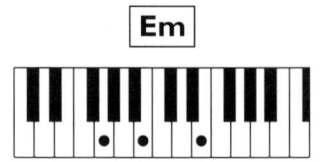

Voice: Electric Guitar

Rhythm: Hard Rock

Tempo: ♩ = 124

G
1. Asked a girl what she want - ed to be,____
2. I told the girl that my pros - pects were good,____
3. I told that girl I could start right a - way,____

C

G **C** **G**
she said, "Ba - by, can't you see?__ I wan-na be fam-ous, a
she said, "Ba - by, it's un - der - stood. Work-ing for pea-nuts is
and she said, "Lis-ten, babe, I've got some-thing to say, I've got no car, and it's

C **D**
star of the screen,__ but you can do some - thing in be - tween."__
all ver - y fine,____ but I can show you a bet - ter time."__
break-ing my heart,____ but I've found a driv - er, and that's a start."__

Em **C** **Em**
Ba - by, you can drive my car,____ yes I'm gon - na be a star,__

ba-by, you can drive my car,____ and may-be I'll love

_____ you.

Beep beep mm beep beep,   yeah!_

Guitar solo

_____

Ba-by, you can drive my   car,____   yes I'm gon-na be a   star,_

ba-by, you can drive my   car,____   and may-be I'll love_

D.C. al Coda
(Verse 3)

Coda

_____ you.

_____ you.

Repeat and fade

Beep beep, mm beep beep,   yeah!____

ELEANOR RIGBY

Words & Music by John Lennon & Paul McCartney

C   Em

Voice: **Strings/Piano (Layer)**

Rhythm: **Pop Ballad**

Tempo: ♩ = 122

Ah,_____ look at all____ the lone - ly peo - ple!

Ah,_____ look at all____ the lone - ly peo

- ple!

1. El - ea - nor Rig - by,   picks up the rice____ in the church
2. Fa - ther Mac - Ken - zie,   writ - ing the words____ of a ser -
3. El - ea - nor Rig - by,   died in the church____ and was bur -

—— where a wed - ding has been,____   lives in a dream.____
- mon that no - one will hear,____   no - one comes near.____
- ied a - long____ with her name,____   no - bod - y came.____

Waits at the win - dow,
Look at him work - ing,
Fa - ther Mac - Ken - zie,

wear - ing the face___ that she keeps___
darn - ing his socks___ in the night___
wip - ing the dirt___ from his hands___

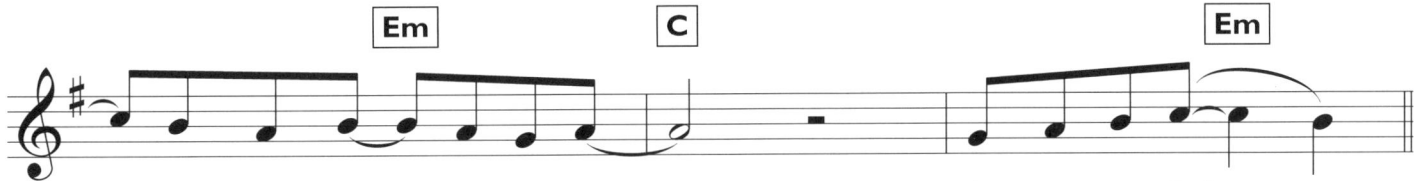

Em   C   Em

___ in a jar___ by the door,___   who is it for?___
___ when there's no - bo-dy there,___   what does he care?___
___ as he walks___ from the grave,___   no - one was saved.___

Em

All the lone - ly peo - ple,   where do___ they all___ come from?___

Em

___ All the lone - ly peo - ple,   where do___

To Coda ⊕ | 1. | 2.   D.C. al Coda

___ they all___ be - long?___

⊕ Coda

Em
Strings

GET BACK

Words & Music by John Lennon & Paul McCartney

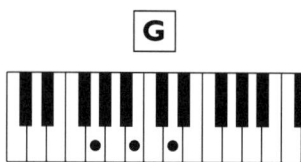
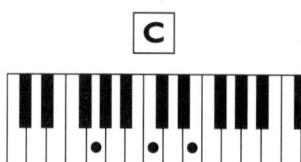
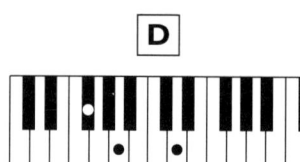

Voice: **Gut Guitar**

Rhythm: **Pop Rock 1**

Tempo: ♩ = 132

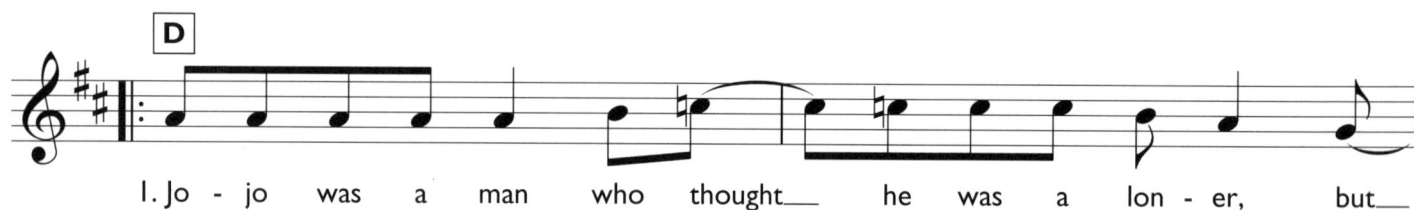

1. Jo - jo was a man who thought___ he was a lon - er, but___

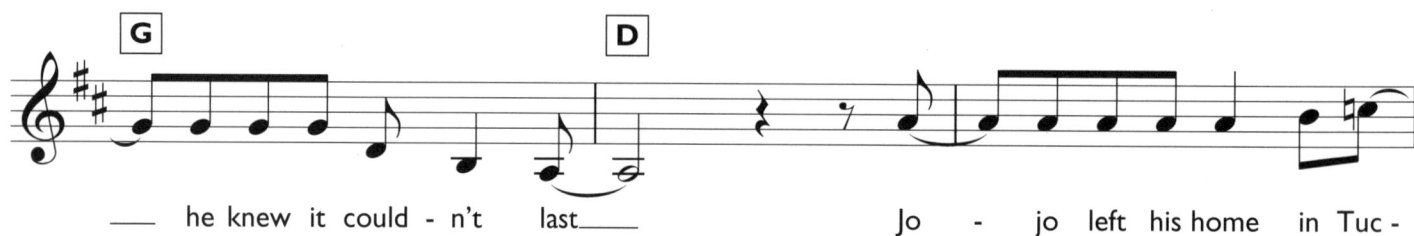

___ he knew it could - n't last___ Jo - jo left his home in Tuc -

- son, Ar - i - zo - na, for___ some Cal - i - for - nia grass.___ Get back!

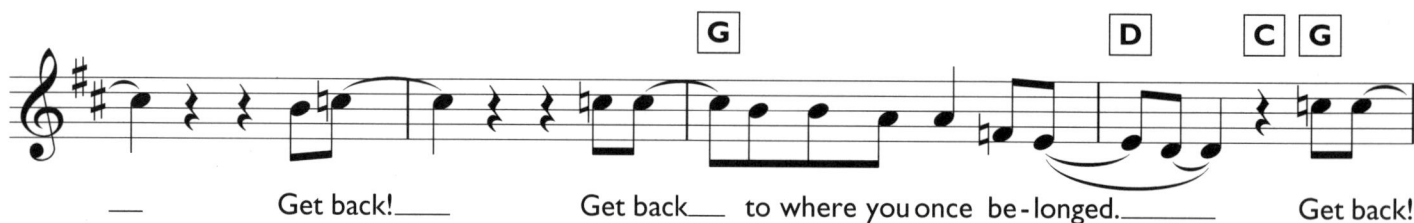

___ Get back!___ Get back___ to where you once be - longed.___ Get back!

Get back!___ Get back___ to where you once be-longed._____(Get back Jo-jo!)

2. Sweet Lor-ret-ta Mar - tin thought___ she was a wo man but___ she was an-oth-er man.

All___ the girls a-round her say___ she's got it com-ing but___

___ she gets it while she can.___ Get back!___ Get back!___ Get back

___ to where you once be - longed._____ Get back!___ Get back!

___ Get back___ to where you once be - longed._____ (Get back)

HELLO GOODBYE

Words & Music by John Lennon & Paul McCartney

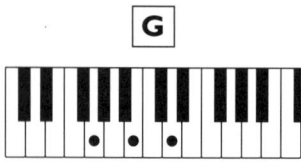

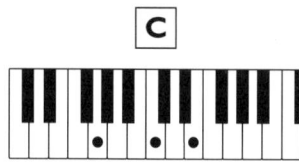

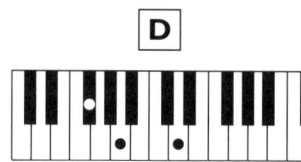

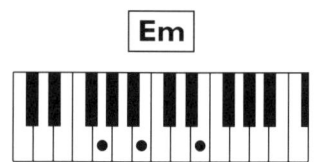

Voice: **Piano**

Rhythm: **Rock 1**

Tempo: ♩ = 102

1. You say yes,___ I say no,___ you say stop,___ but I say go,___ go, go..

___ Oh___ no.___ You say___ good-bye___ and

I say; hel-lo,_____ hel-lo,___ hel-lo,___ I don't___ know

why you say___ good-bye,___ I say hel-lo,_____ hel-lo,___ hel-lo,___

___ I don't know why you say___ good-bye,___ I say hel-lo._____

2. I say high,— you say low,— you say why— and I say I— don't know.—

3. You say yes,— I say no,— you say stop— and I say go,— go, go.—

— Oh— oh— no.— You say— good-bye— and I say hel-lo,—

— hel-lo,— hel-lo,— I don't— know why you say— good-bye,— I say hel-lo,—

— hel - lo,— hel - lo,— I don't— know

To Coda ⊕

why you say— good-bye,— I say hel-lo.—— Why, why, why,

D.S. al Coda

why, why, why— do you say— good-bye,— good-bye?— (bye bye bye bye)

⊕ *Coda*

— Hel-lo,— hel-lo,— I don't— know why you say— good-bye,— I say hel-

Repeat and fade

- lo,—— hel - lo.— He - la, he - ba, hel - lo - a.

17

I'M DOWN

Words & Music by John Lennon & Paul McCartney

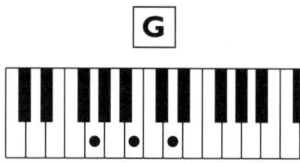

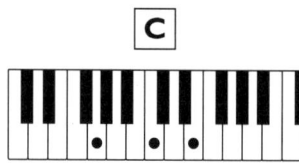

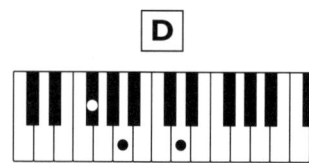

G   C   D

Voice: **Rock Organ**
Rhythm: **Rock & Roll**
Tempo: ♩ = 160

N.C.

1. You tell lies think-in' I can't see,___
2. Man buys ring, wo-man throws it a-way,___
3. We're all a-lone and there's no-bo-dy else,___

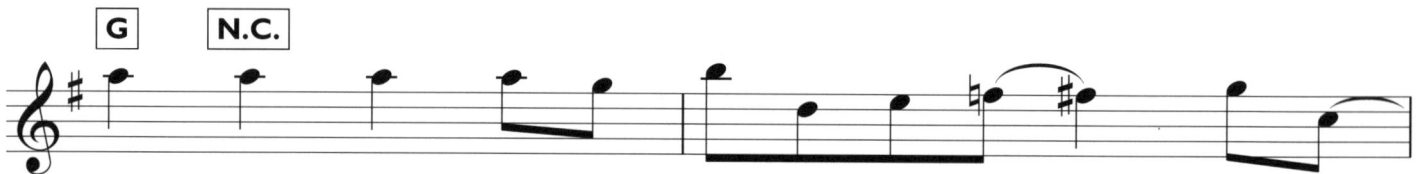

G   **N.C.**

You can't cry, 'cause you're laugh-in' at me.___
Same old thing hap-pens ev-er-y day.___ } I'm down,_
You still moan, "Keep your hands to your-self!"

C

___ (I'm real-ly down,)___

G

I'm down,___ (down on the ground,)_

C

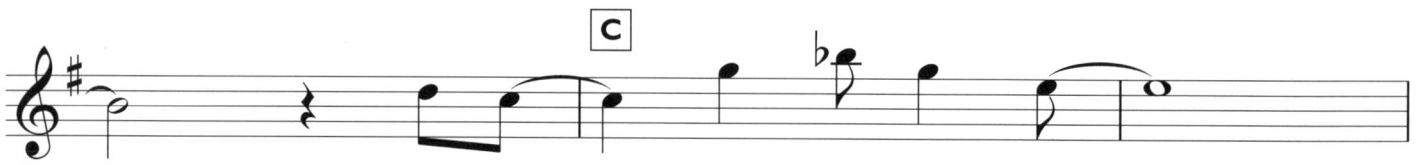

___ I'm down,___ (I'm real-ly down,)___

18

D **G** **N.C.** **D** **G** **N.C.**

How can you laugh___ when you know I'm down?___ (How can you laugh)___ when you

1, 2. **3.**

know I'm down?___ know I'm down?___

G

(I'm real - ly down,)___ Oh yes I'm down,___ (I'm real - ly down,)_

C

___ I'm down on the ground, (I'm real - ly down,)___ I'm___ down,_

G **D**

___ (I'm real - ly down,)___ Ah, ba - by, I'm up - side - down.

C **G** **D** *Repeat and fade*

Oh yeah, yeah,___ yeah,_ yeah,___ yeah._ I'm down.

I'VE JUST SEEN A FACE

Words & Music by John Lennon & Paul McCartney

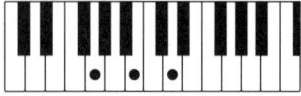 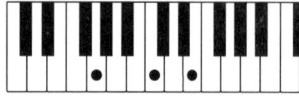 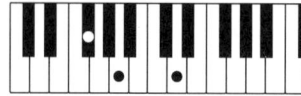 

Voice: **Acoustic Guitar**

Rhythm: **Skiffle Rock**

Tempo: ♩ = 122

I've just seen a face, I can't for-get the time__ or place where we just

met, she's just the girl__ for me and I____ want all the world to see__ we've

To Coda ⊕

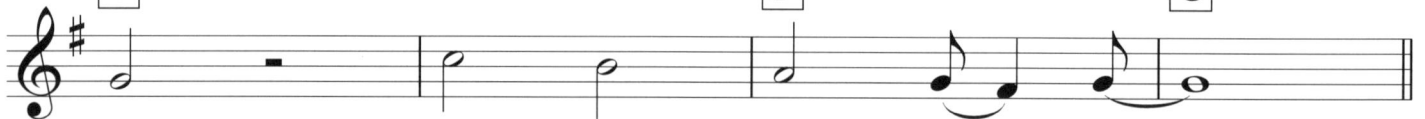

met. Mm mm mm mm__ mm.__

Had it been__ an-oth-er day__ I might have looked the oth-er way__ and
I have nev-er known the like__ of this, I've been a-lone and I__ have

I'd have nev-er been___ a-ware,__ but as it is I'll dream of her__ to-night,
missed things and kept out__ of sight,__ but oth-er girls were nev-er quite__ like this.

Da   da   da   da - da   da.____

Fall - ing,____   yes I am   fall - ing,____

and   she keeps   call - ing____   me   back   a - gain.__

1.   **2.**   *D.C. al Coda*

⊕ Coda

Fall - ing,____   yes I am   fall - ing,____   and she keeps

1, 2.

call - ing____   me   back   a - gain.____

3.

LET IT BE

Words & Music by John Lennon & Paul McCartney

G   C   D   Em

Voice: **Studio Piano**

Rhythm: **Soft Rock I**

Tempo: ♩ = 74

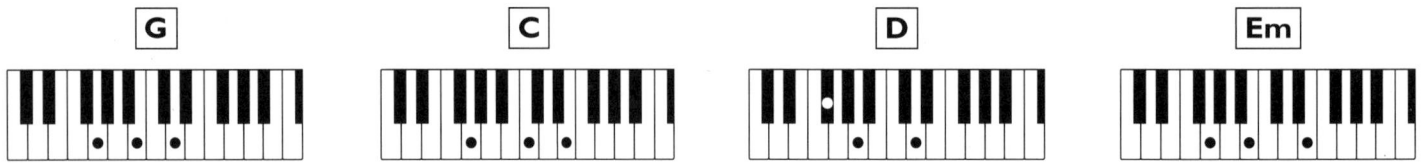

1. When I find my-self in times of trou-ble Mo-ther Ma-ry comes to me,

speak-ing words of wis-dom, let it be.___ And

in my hour of dark-ness, she is stand-ing right in front of me,

speak-ing words of wis-dom, let it be.___ Let it

be,_ let it be, let it be,_____ let it be._

Whis-per words of wis - dom, let it be.____ 2. And

(2.) when the bro - ken heart - ed peo - ple liv - ing in the world a - gree,
(3.) when the night is clou - dy there is still a light that shines on me,

there will be an an - swer, let it be.___ For
shine un - til to - mo - row let it be.___ I

though they may be part - ed there is still a chance that they will see.
wake up to the sound of mus - ic Mo - ther Ma - ry comes to me,

There will be an ans-wer   let it   be.___
speak - ing words of   wis - dom   let it   be.___   Let   it

be   let   it   be,   let   it   be,_____   let   it   be._

There will   be   an   ans - wer,   let   it   be.___   Oh   let   it

be,   let   it   be,   let   it   be,_____   let   it   be.

Whis-per words of wis-dom   let it   be._____   3. And   be,_____

24

TAXMAN

Words & Music by George Harrison

Voice: **Electric Guitar**

Rhythm: **Beat Rock**

Tempo: ♩ = 130

1. Let me____ tell you____ how it____
(2.) ____ per - cent____ ap - pear_

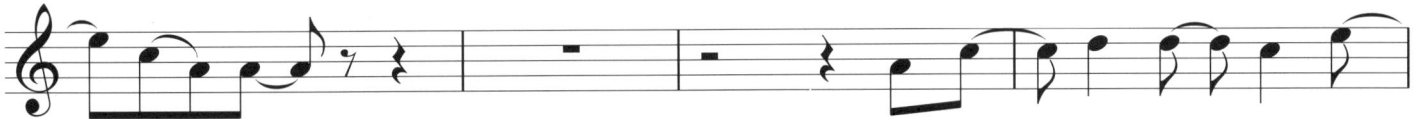

____ will__ be:____   There's one____ for you,_ nine - teen_
____ too_ small,_   be thank - ful I____ don't take_

____ for me,_   'Cause I'm the Tax - man,_   yeah,____ I'm the
____ it__ all._

____ Tax - man.____   2. Should five   (If you drive_

_____ a car,) I'll tax_____ the street, (If you try_____ to sit,)_____ I'll tax_

C   **D**

_____ your_ seat,_ (If you get_____ too cold,)_ I'll tax_____ the heat._ (If you take_

C

_____ a walk,) I'll_____ tax_____ your_ feet._

D   **C**

Tax - man!_____   'Cause I'm the Tax - man,_____

G   **D**

yeah,_____ I'm the_____ Tax - man._____

3. Don't ask_____ me what_ I want_ it for._

(Ah - ah,_____ Mis - ter Wil - son!)_ If you_ don't want_ to pay_

_____ some more._____ (Ah - ah_____ Mis - ter Heath.)_____ 'Cause I'm the

C ..... **G**

Tax - man,_____ yeah,_____ I'm the_____ Tax - man._____

D

_____ 4. Now my_____ ad - vice_____ for those_____ who die,_____

(Tax - man!)_____ De - clare_____ the pen - nies on_____ your_ eyes._

C

(Tax - man!)_____ 'Cause I'm the Tax - man,_____

G ..... **D**

yeah,_____ I'm the_____ Tax - man,_____ and you're_

N.C. ..... **D**

_____ work - ing for no - one but_ me. (Taxman!)

LOVE ME DO

Words & Music by John Lennon & Paul McCartney

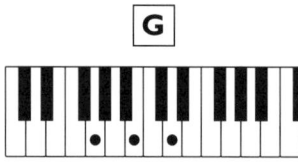

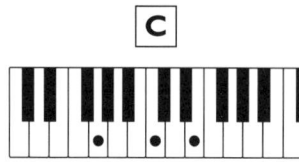

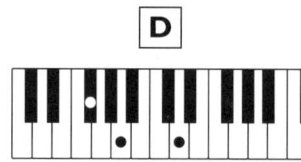

Voice: **Electric Guitar**

Rhythm: **4 Beat Rock**

Tempo: = 138

Love, love me do, you know I love you,

I'll al - ways be true, so

please love me do.

Oh, love me do.

Some - one to love, some - bod - y new.

Some - one to love, some - one like you.

Love, love me do,_____ you know I love you,__

___ I'll al - ways be true,____ so

please_____ love me do.____

D.C. al Coda

Oh,_____ love____ me do.____

⊕ *Coda*

Repeat and fade

Oh,_____ love____ me do.____

OB-LA-DI, OB-LA-DA

Words & Music by John Lennon & Paul McCartney

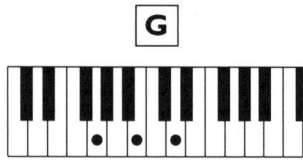

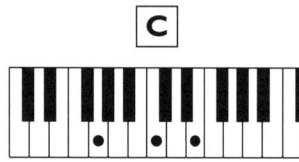

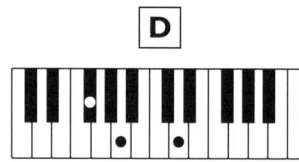

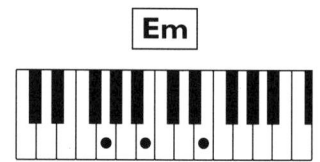

Voice: **Honky Tonk Piano**

Rhythm: **Rock 2**

Tempo: ♩ = 112

1. Des-mond has a bar-row in the mar-ket place,___ Mol-
2. Des-mond takes a trol-ley to the jewel-ler's store,___ buys_

- ly is a sing-er in a band. Des-
___ a twen-ty car-at gold-en ring. Takes_

- mond says to Mol-ly, "Girl I like your face",___ and Mol-ly
___ it back to Mol-ly wait-ing at the door,___ and as he

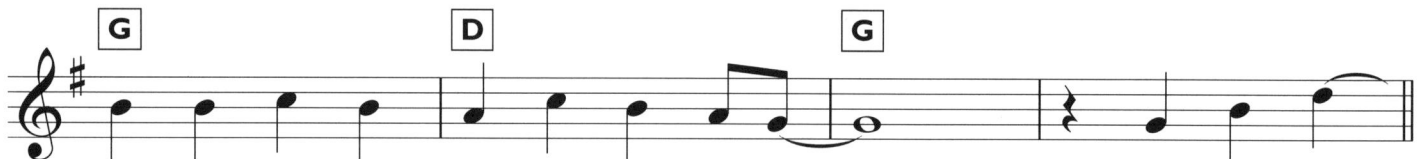

says this as she takes him by the hand.___)
gives it to her, she be-gins to sing:___)

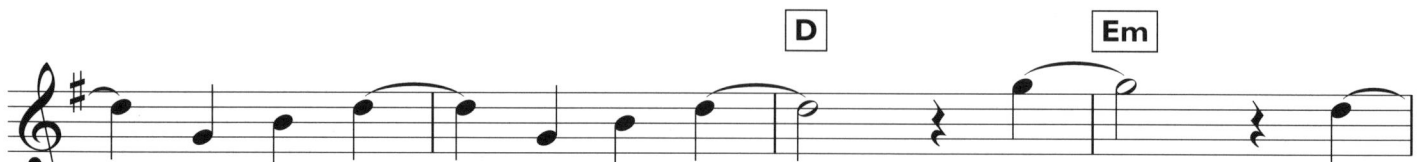

Ob-La-Di,___

Ob-La-Da,___ life goes on,___ bra,___ La-

- la how their life goes on._____ Ob - La - Di,____

_____ Ob - La - Da,_____ life goes on,_____ bra,_____ La -

- la how their life goes on.____

1. 2.

In a cou - ple of years, they have built a home__

___ sweet home.____

With a cou - ple of kids run - ning in the yard__

__ of Des - mond and Mol - ly Jones.____

3. Hap - py ev - er af - ter in the mar - ket place,_____ Des -
4. Hap - py ev - er af - ter in the mar - ket place,_____ Mol -

G

-mond lets the child-ren lend a hand.
-ly lets the child-ren lend a hand.

Mol-

C

-ly stays at home and does her pret-ty face,_____ and in the

G   **D**   **G**

eve-ning she still sings it with the band._____ Ob - La - Di,___

D   **Em**

___ Ob - La - Da,_____ life goes on,_____ bra,_____ La -

G   **D**   **G**

- la how their life goes on._____ Ob - La - Di,___

D   **Em**

___ Ob - La - Da,_____ life goes on,_____ bra,_____ La -

1.   2.

G   **D**   **G**   **Em**

- la how their life goes on._____ ___ And if you

D   **G**

want some fun,___ take Ob - La - Di - Bla - Da.

OCTOPUS'S GARDEN

Words & Music by Ringo Starr

G   **C**   **D**   **Em**

Voice: **Honky Tonk Piano**

Rhythm: **Rock 2**

Tempo: ♩ = **140**

G ... **Em**

1. I'd like to be ___ un - der the sea ___ in an

C ... **D**

oct - o - pus - 's gar - den in the shade.

G ... **Em**

He'd let us in, ___ knows where we've been, ___ in his

C ... **D**

oct - o - pus - 's gar - den in the shade.

Em

I'd ask my friends to come and see ___

an oct - o - pus - 's gar - den with me._____

I'd like to be_____ un - der the sea_____ in an

oct - o - pus - 's gar - den in the shade.__

2. We would be warm____ be - low__ the storm____ in our
3. We would shout__ and swim a - bout____ the

lit - tle__ hide a - way__ be-neath the waves.__
cor - al_____ that lies be-neath the waves.__

Rest - ing our head__ on the sea bed__ in an
Oh, what joy____ for ev - 'ry girl and boy,__

oct - o - pus - 's gar - den near a cave.
know - ing they're hap - py and they're safe.

We would sing and dance a - round,_____
We would be so hap - py, you and me,_____

be - cause we know we can't be found.
no - one there to tell us what to do.

I'd like to be____ un - der the sea____ in an

oct - o - pus - 's gar - den in the shade.____

⊕ Coda

____ in an oct - o - pus - 's gar - den with you,____

in an oct - o - pus - 's gar - den with you.____

in an oct - o - pus - 's gar - den with you.____

PAPERBACK WRITER

Words & Music by John Lennon & Paul McCartney

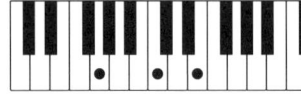

Voice: **Distorted Guitar**

Rhythm: **Rock I**

Tempo: ♩ = 156

Pa - per-back wri - ter, pa - per-back wri - ter.

1. Dear_____

Sir or Mad-am, will you read my book, it took me years to write,_ will you
(3.) thou - sand pag - es, give or take a few, I'll be writ - ing more_ in a

take a look? It's based on a nov - el by a man named Lear, and I
week or two. I can make it long - er if you like the style, I can

need a job,___ so I want to be a pa - per-back wri - ter,_____
change it round,_ and I want to be a pa - per-back wri - ter,_____

G

_ pa - per - back wri - ter._____ 2. It's a
_ pa - per - back wri - ter._____ 4. If you

dir - ty sto - ry of a dir - ty man,__ and his cling - ing wife__ does-n't
real - ly like it, you can have the rights,__ It could make a mil - lion for you

un - der-stand. His son is work - ing for the *Dai - ly Mail*,__ it's a
ov - er - night. If you must re - turn__ it, you can send it here,__ but I

C

stead - y job,__ but he wants to be a pa - per - back wri - ter,_____
need a break__ and I want to be a pa - per - back wri - ter,_____

G

_ pa - per - back wri - ter._____
_ pa - per - back wri - ter._____

1.
G

N.C.

Pa - per-back wri - ter, pa - per-back wri - ter.

2.
G

3. It's a

G

Repeat and fade

Pa - per - back wri - ter._____

37

RAIN

Words & Music by John Lennon & Paul McCartney

G **C** **D**

Voice:	**Electric Guitar**
Rhythm:	**Hard Rock**
Tempo:	♩ = 112

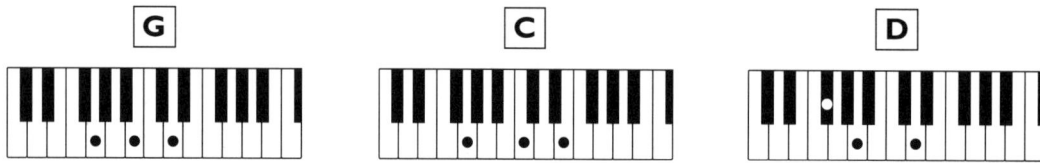

1. If the rain comes, they run and hide their heads. They
(2.) sun shines, they slip in - to the shade And

might as well be dead, if the rain comes,____ if the
sip their lem - on - ade, when the sun shines,____ when the

1.
rain comes. 2. When the

2.
sun shines.

Rain,____

38

I don't mind._____ Shine,_____ the wea-ther's fine.__ _____

3. I can show you that when it starts to
4. Can you hear me that when it rains and

rain, Ev - 'ry - thing's the same, I can show you,_____
shines, It's just a state of mind? Can you hear me?_____

I can show you.
Can you hear me?

TELL ME WHAT YOU SEE

Words & Music by John Lennon & Paul McCartney

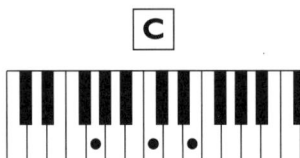

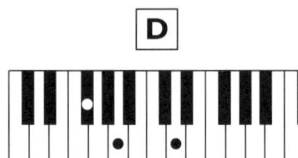

G   C   D

Voice: **Electric Piano**

Rhythm: **Bossa Nova**

Tempo: ♩ = 138

G	C	D	G

1. If you let___ me take___ your heart,___
2. Big and black___ the clouds___ may be,___
3. Lis - ten to___ me one___ more time,___

	C	G

I will prove___ to you,___
time will pass___ a - way,___
how can I___ get through?___

	C	D	G

we will nev - er be___ a - part,___
if you put___ your trust___ in me,___
Can't you try___ to see___ that I'm___

C	D	G

if I'm part___ of you.
I'll make bright___ your day.
trying to get___ to you?___

40

O - pen up_____ your eyes_____ now,_____
Look in - to_____ these eyes_____ now,_____
O - pen up_____ your eyes_____ now,_____

tell me what_____ you see,_____
tell me what_____ you see,_____
tell me what_____ you see,_____

it is no_____ sur - prise_____ now,_____
don't you re - a - lise,_____ now,_____
it is no_____ sur - prise_____ now,_____

1.

what you see____ is me._____
what you see____ is me?__
what you see____ is me.__

2.

Tell me what you see.____

3.

____ Mmm mmm mmm mmm mmm.

THANK YOU GIRL

Words & Music by John Lennon & Paul McCartney

G · C · D · Em

Voice: **Drawbar Organ**

Rhythm: **Hard Rock**

Tempo: ♩ = 138

D · C · D · C

Oh,   oh,

G · C · G · C · G · D

1. You've been good to me, you made me glad when I was
2. I could tell the world a thing or two a-bout our

G · C · G · C · G · C

blue.   And e-ter-nal-ly, I'll al-ways
love.   I know lit-tle girl, on-ly a

G · D · G · C

be in love with you,⎫
fool would doubt our love,⎭ and all I got-ta

To Coda ⊕ | 1. | 2.

D **C** **D** **D**

do   is   thank   you   girl;___   thank   you   girl.___   thank   you,   girl.___

Em **G** **D**

Thank   you   girl   for   lov - ing   me   the   way   that you do,   (way   that you do,)

Em **D** **G**

that's   the   kind   of   love   that   is   too   good   to   be   true,   and

C **D** **C** **D** *D.C. al Coda*

all   I   got - ta   do   is   thank   you   girl;___   thank   you   girl.___

⊕ *Coda*

D **C**

thank   you   girl.___

D **C** **G** **C** **G** **C**

Oh,   oh,   oh!

D **C** **G**

Oh,   oh!

43

TWIST AND SHOUT

Words & Music by Bert Russell & Phil Medley

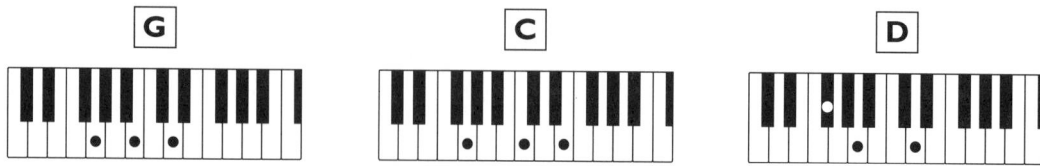

Voice: **Electric Guitar**

Rhythm: **Rock & Roll**

Tempo: ♩ = 120

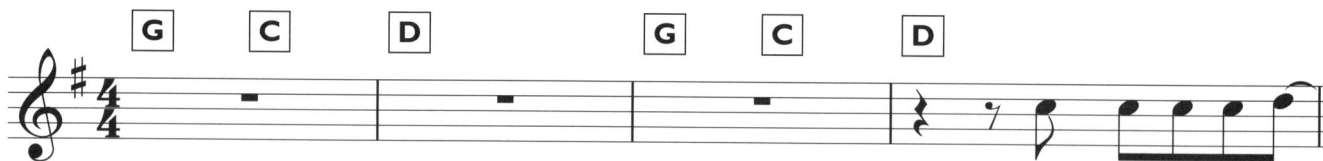

Well, shake it up, ba-

-by,— now, (shake it up, ba - by,) Twist and shout, (twist and shout.)

C' mon,— c' mon, c' mon,— c' mon ba - by— now, (come on ba -

-by,) Come on and work it on out,_____ (work it on out.)—

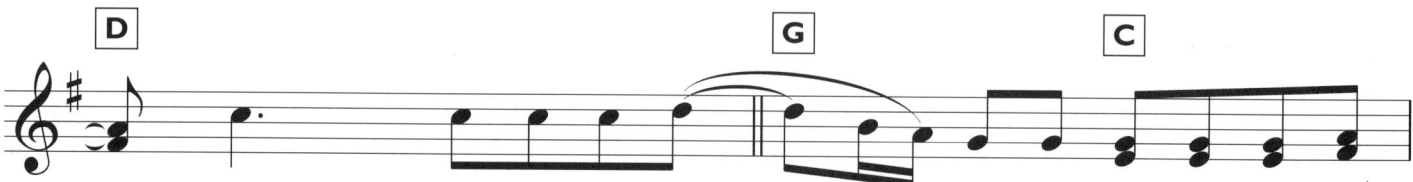

___ 1. Well, work it on out,_____ hon - ey, (work it on out,)
2. 3. You know you twist it, lit - tle girl,_____ (twist lit - tle girl,)

D | **G** | **C**

You know you look so good, (look so good.)
You know you twist so fine, (twist so fine.)

D | **G** | **C**

You know you got me go - in'___ now, (got me go -
Come on and twist a lit - tle clos - er___ now, (twist a lit-tle clo -

D | **G** | *To Coda* | **C**

- in',) Just like I knew___ you would,___ (like I knew you would,
-ser,) And let me know___ that you're mine, (let me know you're mine,

1. | **2.** | *Play 4 times*

D | **D** | **G** | **C** | **D** | **C**

ooh!) Well, shake it up, ba - ooh!)

D.S. al Coda

D

Ah,_____ ah,_____ ah._____ Shake it up, ba -

Coda

D | **G** | **C** | **D**

Well, shake it, shake it, shake it ba - by___ now, Well, shake it, shake it, shake it

G | **C** | **D** | **G** | **C**

ba - by___ now,___ Well, shake it, shake it, shake it, ba - by___ now.

D | **G**

Ah,_____ ah,_____

YELLOW SUBMARINE

Words & Music by John Lennon & Paul McCartney

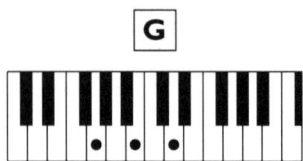

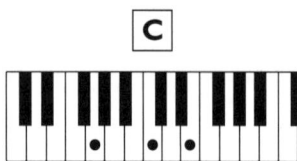

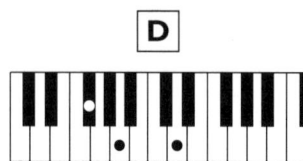

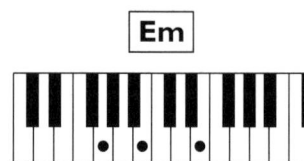

G   C   D   Em

Voice: **Banjo**

Rhythm: **Slow Rock I**

Tempo: ♩ = 120

1. In the town_____ where I was born, lived a man_____ who sailed to sea, and he told_____ us of his life, in the land_____ of sub - ma - rines. 2. So we sailed_____ up to the sun, till we

Lyrics under the staves:

found_____ the sea of green, and we lived_____ be-neath the

waves, in our yel - low sub - ma - rine.

We all live in a yel - low sub - ma - rine,

yel - low sub - ma - rine, yel - low sub - ma - rine.

We all live in a yel - low sub - ma - rine,

yel - low sub - ma - rine, yel - low sub - ma - rine. 3. And our

friends_____ are all a - board, ma - ny more of them live next

D | **G** | **D** | **C** | **G** | **Em**

door, and the band_____ be -gins to play.

C | **D** | **G** | **G**

We all live in a

D | **G**

yel - low sub - ma-rine, yel - low sub - ma-rine, yel - low sub - ma-rine.

G | **D**

We all live in a yel - low sub - ma-rine, yel - low sub - ma-rine,

G | **D** | **C** | **G** | **Em**

yel - low sub - ma-rine. 4. As we live a life of ease, ev - 'ry

C | **D** | **G** | **D** | **C**

one of us has all we need, sky of blue and sea of

G | **Em** | **C** | **D** | *D.S. and fade*

green, in our yel - low sub - ma - rine.

2 3 4 5 6 7 8 9
1/10 (172712)